**Great British Wo**men

*who deserve greater re*c

# Knocking at the Gates

*'Making space for women in the stories we tell about the past can help make space for women in the stories we tell about our future'*

*Anita Sarkeesian and Laura Hudson, 'We Must Rewrite Women's Role in History', TIME, March 2016*

This book brings together 100 Great British women who made their mark and yet all deserve greater recognition. None of them are as yet represented within the photographs, prints, paintings, drawings or sculptures of nearly 17,000 women who currently feature within the greatest visual celebration of Great British history that is the Collection of the National Portrait Gallery, London. Their stories, in very brief biographical entries, are sorted by the professional categories in which these women made their names.

David Saywell

© 2016 David Saywell
Printed by CreateSpace
ISBN-13: 978-1539051053
ISBN-10: 1539051056
Visit great-british.co.uk to order additional copies
Follow me on Twitter @britishprints

For Leonie and you championing the writing back
into history the achievements of women

# Margaret Costa
1917 – 1999
Restaurateur and writer on cookery

**Margaret Costa** (30 August 1917 – 1 August 1999) was a restaurateur and writer on cookery. Her career began writing recipes for the *Sunday Pictorial* during the war and in the 1950s cooked at dinner parties in people's homes and contributed to early editions of the *Good Food Guide*. In 1965 Costa became the cookery writer for the *Sunday Times* and in 1970 published *The Four Seasons Cookery Book*, including dinner-party classics such as chilled avocado soup and duck with orange sauce. She said that 'her first husband insisted she cook only English food, the second only French whilst the third cooked for her'. She and third husband Bill Lacy opened *Lacy's* restaurant in London in 1970 where they experimented charging for the wine *not* drunk from the bottle.

# Pearl Witherington
## 1914 – 2008
### Special operations officer

---

**Pearl Witherington** (24 June 1914 – 24 February 2008) was a special operations officer. She grew up in Paris and was bilingual in French. Returning to London in 1940 she worked in the Air Ministry before becoming a Special Operations Executive in 1943, learning guerilla and sabotage skills and recognised for her shooting skills. Parachuted into occupied France, she worked for Maurice Southgate of the Stationer network, disguised as a cosmetics saleswoman. When Southgate was captured she led the Wrestler network with her fiancé, building up a private army of 3,000. Her network ambushed road convoys during the D-Day landings and forced the surrender of 18,000 retreating German troops, for which she was awarded the French Légion d'honneur.

---

Armed Forces and Intelligence Services

# Cicely Mary Barker

1895 – 1973

Artist and writer

**Cicely Mary Barker** (28 June 1895 – 16 February 1973) was an artist and writer. Schooled at home as she suffered from epilepsy, Barker was inspired by artists like Kate Greenaway in books read in her nursery library and from 1908 enrolled in classes at Croydon Art Society. In 1923 her *Flower Fairies of the Spring* was published, followed by books for the Summer and Autumn in 1925 and 1926. She used children in her sister's kindergarten at the family home as models for her books and designed the flower fair costumes for the children to wear based on the flowers and plants she illustrated. Faith underpinned all her work and Barker also executed paintings for churches and chapels and wrote *The Children's Book of Hymns* and *He Leadeth Me*.

# Margaret Belsky
1919 – 1989
Cartoonist and illustrator

**Margaret Belsky** (20 June 1919 – 26 January 1989) was a cartoonist and illustrator. After winning a *Punch* competition at Bournemouth School of Art she studied illustration at the Royal College of Art, meeting and marrying in 1944 a Czech soldier, Franta Belsky, who later became a well-known sculptor. Her first cartoons appeared in *Lilliput* magazine and in 1951 she joined the *Daily Herald* to became the first woman to draw a front-page cartoon for a national newspaper. She contributed 6,500 cartoons over 18 years for the *Herald* and *Sun* as it was renamed after 1964. Additionally she illustrated children's books as well as book jackets for Penguin.

Art

# Clarice Cliff

1899 – 1972

Ceramic designer and art director

**Clarice Cliff** (20 January 1899 – 23 October 1972) was a ceramic designer and art director. In 1916 she joined pottery manufacturer Arthur J. Wilkinson Ltd; her talent was recognised, so much so that by 1925 Cliff was given her own studio at Newport Pottery. In 1927 she developed the Bizarre range, brightly coloured, Art Deco in style and immediately popular, and branched out into geometrical shapes in designs such as Conical and Bon Jour. In 1928 she produced the Crocus pattern that remained in production until 1963. From 1929 until the mid-1930s her designs were bold, and used solid areas of bright colour in designs ranging from abstract to stylised flowers and fruit. She achieved enormous success during this period.

# Evelyn Dunbar

1906 – 1960

Painter

---

**Evelyn Dunbar** (18 December 1906 – 12 May 1960) was a painter. She studied at the Royal College of Art from 1929 to 1933 and was one of a group of graduates commissioned to provide murals for Brockley County School, depicting scenes from Aesop's *Fables*. She enjoyed gardening subjects and worked with Cyril Mahoney on book illustrations for *Gardener's Choice*. During the war she became an official war artist, concentrating on the Women's Land Army and hospital and nursing paintings. She worked in her native Kent and it was Strood in Rochester that provided the setting for her painting *The Queue at the Fish-Shop* using her favoured long horizontal format. After the war she painted portraits, landscapes and allegorical pictures.

Art

# Jessie King
1875 – 1949
Illustrator and designer

**Jessie King** (20 March 1875 – 3 August 1849) was an illustrator and designer. She studied at Glasgow School of Art from 1892 to 1899, where, working in pen and ink and watercolour, she developed her drawing style, characterised by patterned surface, elongated lines and arabesque forms in lettered frames. From 1899 to 1902 she was commissioned to illustrate a series of book covers by Globus Verlag in Berlin whilst teaching book decoration and design at the School of Art. From 1905 she also designed fabrics and jewellery. Her fantasy worlds favoured fairies, sailing ships and spiders webs all drawn with a meticulous attention to detail.

# Nancy Lancaster
## 1897 – 1994
### Interior decorator

**Nancy Lancaster** (10 September 1897 – 19 August 1994) was an American-born interior decorator. She bought into the decorating firm Colefax and Fowler, and alongside John Fowler was responsible for what became the English country-house look. Nancy Astor was an aunt and Joyce Grenfell a cousin, and Nancy married Ronald Tree in 1920. It was with improving the houses they owned, including Ditchley Park in Oxfordshire, that her lifelong passion developed. Her philosophy of taste centred around elegance and comfort and never making a room look decorated. Flowers, fabrics and antiques combined with open fires to create the look. She and Fowler worked on many English country houses and gardens including Arundel, Badminton and Boughton.

Art

# Frances Macdonald

1873 – 1921

Artist

**Frances Macdonald** (24 August 1873 – 12 December 1921) was an artist and one of the Glasgow Four. She and her sister Margaret began taking classes at Glasgow School of Art in 1891. There Frances met her future husband Herbert McNair and Margaret her husband Charles Rennie Mackintosh, labelled 'the spooky school' and defined the Glasgow Style. Frances and Margaret set up a studio, working together on textile designs, illustrations and metalwork marked with Celtic, mystical and symbolic imagery. In 1899 she and McNair married and moved to Liverpool where collaborations included a Writing Room for the International Exhibition of Modern Art in Turin. She produced watercolours focussed on marriage and motherhood in later years. Her husband destroyed many of her works after her death.

Art

# Syrie Maugham
### 1879 – 1955
### Interior decorator

**Syrie Maugham** (10 July 1879 – 25 July 1955) was an interior decorator. Daughter of Thomas Barnado, founder of the charity Barnados, she began a relationship with Somerset Maugham in 1913 when separated but not divorced from wealthy pharmaceutical manufacturer Sir Henry Wellcome. After an apprenticeship with a decorating firm she set up her own business in 1922. She became known for her white rooms with accents of colour, plaster palm fronds, sea shell motifs and mirrored screens, moving on in the 1930s to bright greens and shocking pinks. Clients included Noel Coward (for whom she decorated both town and country houses), Wallis Simpson, Edward James, Stephen Tennant and Edward VIII with the 1936 Fort Belvedere commission.

# Jessie Newbery
## 1864 – 1948
### Artist and embroiderer

**Jessie Newbery** (28 May 1864 – 27 April 1948) was an artist and embroiderer. In 1884 she went to study at the Glasgow School of Art after becoming interested in textiles on a trip to Italy. She married the School of Art's director, Francis Newbery, in 1889 and in 1894 was appointed head of its department of embroidery. Her appliqué work was characterised by simple stylized flowers and leaves, cut out of coloured linens and she favoured using light purples, greens, blues and pink. Newbery's rose motif with satin stitch to emulate petal folds was picked up by Margaret and Frances Macdonald and then Charles Rennie Mackintosh with what became known as the Glasgow Style. Newbery also taught dress design and her own designs have an Italian Renaissance look.

Art

# Dorothy Renton

1898 – 1966

Gardener

---

**Dorothy Renton** (7 April 1898 – 28 January 1966) was a gardener. Along with her husband, John Renton, they developed from 1925 three rock gardens linked to Branlyn, a house they built above the banks of the River Tay in Scotland. They were founder members of the Alpine Garden Society and Scottish Rock Garden Club. Dorothy grew most of her plants from seeds collected mainly from Tibet, Bhutan and China, from expeditions led by Joseph Rock (her pink-barked birch from Rock's travels in south-west China won her an international reputation), George Forrest and others. She won the Scottish Rock Garden Club Forrest medal four times. Renton was also a pioneer of peat-wall planting, making it possible for her to grow dwarf acid-loving plants.

Art

# Antonia Yeoman
## 1907 – 1970
### Cartoonist and illustrator

**Antonia Yeoman** (24 July 1907 – 30 June 1970) was a cartoonist and illustrator. Born Beryl Thompson, she became a commercial and fashion artist after studying at the Royal Academy Schools. She took the name 'Antonia' and from 1937 she and brother Harold Thompson produced cartoons, usually in black and white with Indian ink, often of 'elegant men-about-town, superior spivs and the middle classes', under the pseudonym 'Anton'. Their first cartoons appeared in *Night & Day* in 1937 and then *Punch* in 1938. After the war they renewed their partnership till Harold's work as a director of an advertising agency left him less time for drawing. All the 'Antons' after 1949 for the *Daily Telegraph, Tatler, New Yorker* and *Private Eye* were by Antonia.

Art

# Ellenor Fenn

1744 – 1813

Educationist and children's writer

---

**Ellenor Fenn** (12 March 1744 – 1 November 1813) was an educationist and children's writer. In 1766 she married John Fenn, but they remained childless. Her interest in literature developed as she wrote, illustrated and bound books for nieces and nephews. From 1782 to 1812 she published prolifically anonymously or under the pseudonyms Mrs Teachwell or Mrs Lovechild. Her most famous book is *Cobwebs to Catch Flies* focussed on helping teach children reading skills. She was particularly interested in educating girls, publishing much in the series *Mrs Teachwell's Library for Young Ladies*, and providing mothers with the materials and confidence to help teach their children. Her works were popular in their day and regularly reprinted up to the 1870s.

# Louisa Gurney

1784 – 1836

Diarist and educationist

**Louisa Gurney** (25 September 1784 – 6 September 1836) was a diarist and educationist from the Gurney Quaker family. She married the banker Samuel Hoare in 1806 and joined her siblings championing various causes including prison reform with her sister Elizabeth Fry, anti-slavery campaigns, and founded the *Ladies' Society for Promoting Education in the West Indies*. Following the lead of her mother Catherine Bell, she concerned herself with the education of parents to raise their own children in two books: *Hints for the Improvement of Early Education and Nursery Discipline* in 1819 and *Friendly Advice on the Management and Education of Children, Addressed to Parents of the Middle and Labouring Classes of Society* in 1824.

Education and Learning

# Violet Carson

1898 – 1983

Actress

**Violet Carson** (1 September 1898 – 26 December 1983) was an English actress most well-known for her portrayal of Ena Sharples in *Coronation Street*. She learned the piano as a child, forming the Carson Sisters with her sister Nellie and as a teenager became a cinema pianist accompanying silent films. From 1935 she began a career in radio, singing a wide repertoire in the show *Songs at the Piano* and then appeared in *Children's Hour*, acted in radio dramas and even become a presenter and interviewer on *Woman's Hour*. From 1960 to 1980 she appeared as the belligerent old woman Ena Sharples in *Coronation Street*, noted for her hairnet and sharp tongue, often seen drinking milk stout in *The Rovers Return*, putting the world to rights.

# Ivy Close
## 1890 – 1968
### Beauty queen and film actress

**Ivy Close** (15 June 1890 – 4 December 1968) was a film actress. In 1908 she won Britain's first national beauty contest, organised by the *Daily Mirror*, defeating 15,000 other contestants. She married Elwin Neane, a portrait photographer commissioned by the newspaper to photograph the contestants. He also directed her in her first film *Dream Paintings* in 1912 in which she posed as figures in famous paintings, and together they formed Ivy Close Films in 1914. Her first feature film was *Lure of London* in 1916, then appeared in *The Women's Land Army*, as Nelson's wife in the propaganda film *Nelson* in 1918 and in Abel Gance's pioneering French film *La Roue* in 1920. Thereafter her career stagnated with the arrival of the talkies in the 1920s.

Film and Broadcasting

# Fanny Cradock
1909 – 1984
Television chef

**Fanny Cradock** (26 February 1909 – 27 December 1984) was a television chef. Marriages, divorces, separations and an annulment preceeded meeting her fourth husband Major Johnnie Cradock in 1939 (they married in 1977). They wrote in the *Daily Telegraph* from 1950 to 1955 under the name of 'Bon Viveur' and developed a theatre cooking stage act of a ferocious wife and hen-pecked husband. She began making cookery shows for the BBC from 1955, noted for her French and decorated food. Her cookery books sold in record numbers, but she was criticised by some for her outdated food, heavy make up and chiffon ballgowns. She was fired by the BBC in 1976 after making disparaging comments about the cooking of the housewife winner of an national cookery competition.

# Patricia Hayes
1909 – 1998
Actress

**Patricia Hayes** (22 December 1909 – 19 September 1998) was an actress. By the age of six she was appearing in seaside shows and by twelve had made her stage debut. In 1928 Hayes won the Bancroft gold medal at the Royal Academy of Dramatic Art, and she established her reputation as the maid in *When we are Married* in 1938. She began to do radio comedy in *Hoop-La* and *Our Shed* during the war and in the late 1940s began supporting comedians, first Ted Ray in *Ray's a Laugh* for 6 years, then Arthur Askey, and Tony Hancock in the latter's *Hancock's Half Hour*. In the 1960s she played Min in *Till Death Us Do Part* and later *In Sickness and in Health*. In 1971 Hayes won a BAFTA for best actress in her role in *Edna, the Inebriate Woman*.

# Hattie Jacques
1922 – 1980
Actress

---

**Hattie Jacques** (7 February 1922 – 6 October 1980) was an actress. She appeared in 1950 with Tony Hancock in *Educating Archie*, written by Eric Sykes and then in *Hancock's Half Hour*. In 1960 she formed a long-standing working relationship as Eric Sykes' twin in the sitcom *Sykes*. Jacques is most well known for her roles in the *Carry On* films. Her first appearance was as a strict medical officer in *Carry on Sergeant* in 1958, and made her first outing as Matron in *Carry on Nurse* in 1959. Her favourite role was the neglected wife of taxi driver Sid James in *Carry on Cabby* in 1963, where she played a romantic lead and set up her own all-woman taxi firm. From 1949 to 1965 she was married to actor John le Mesurier.

---

Film and Broadcasting

# Pat Phoenix

1923 – 1986

Actress

**Pat Phoenix** (26 November 1923 – 17 September 1986) was an actress. Following an early career with minor parts in films, theatre and writing, she nearly gave up acting until she landed the role of brash divorcée Elsie Tanner in *Coronation Street*. She changed her surname from Pilkington to Phoenix, after the mythological bird that rose from the ashes, and then starred in the first episode in December 1960, and featured in 1,641 episodes from 1960 to 1973 and again from 1976 to 1984. Three-times married, she wed screen husband Alan Browning in 1972 and both left the programme; however, she returned and separated from Browning. A heavy smoker, she died of lung cancer six days after she married her long-time companion, actor Tony Booth.

Film and Broadcasting

# Kay Walsh
1911 – 2005
Actress

**Kay Walsh** (15 November 1911 – 16 April 2005) was an actress. Spotted in a play by a film scout, Walsh appeared in many Ealing Studio films during the 1930s. During *Secret of Stamboul* in 1936 she met David Lean, and they were married in 1940. He helped her obtain some of her finest parts he directed, but she more than helped him back, feeding him ideas for future films, as on *Great Expectations*, dialogue for *Pygmalion*, ideas for *Oliver Twist* as well as recommending Anthony Newley to play the Artful Dodger. She also appeared in Lean's *In Which We Serve* and *This Happy Breed* during the 1940s. Their marriage broke down but she enjoyed more success in the 1950s in *Stage Fright*, *Lease of Life* and *The Horse's Mouth*.

# Margaret Damer Dawson

## 1873 – 1920

### Co-founder of the Women's Police Service

**Margaret Damer Dawson** (12 June 1873 – 18 May 1920) was the co-founder of the Women's Police Service. Dawson campaigned against the trafficking of women and children, and for women police to protect women from prostitution and the abuse of children. After serving on the Criminal Law Amendment Committee in 1914 she set up the Women's Police Volunteers with Nina Boyle. They were asked to resolve issues and impose a curfew in Grantham in November that year. A name change followed and in 1916 Dawson was asked to supervise women munition workers during the Great War, supplying and training 140 women. When she died in 1920 leadership of the service was taken over by her professional and personal partner Mary Sophia Allen.

Law and Crime

# Ivy Williams

1877 – 1966

First woman barrister in England

---

**Ivy Williams** (7 September 1877 – 18 February 1966) was the first woman to be called to the English bar in 1922. The daughter of a solicitor, she also had a barrister brother who died during the Great War. She completed her studies at the Society of Oxford Home Students, passed all her exams by 1903 but was unable to matriculate at Oxford until 1920 because of restrictions on women students. In that year women were admitted into the inns of court, and she was called to the bar two years later. She taught law at the Society of Oxford Home Students from 1920 to 1945. In later years as her eyesight began to fail, she taught herself how to read braille and wrote a braille primer published by the National Institute for the Blind in 1948.

# Caroline Biggs
1840 – 1889
Novelist and campaigner for women's suffrage

---

**Caroline Biggs** (23 August 1840 – 4 September 1889) was a novelist and campaigner for women's suffrage. She followed the anti-slavery beliefs held by her mother and published *White and Black: a story of the Southern States* in 1862. She headed for London in the 1860s after the death of her mother and became assistant secretary of the London National Society for Women's Suffrage for four years till 1871 and wrote the chapter on Britain in Elizabeth Stanton's *History of Women Suffrage* published in 1887. Her novel *Waiting for Tidings* in 1874 covered the legal status of women in marriage. From 1870 to 1889 she was editor of the *Englishman's Review* and was on the committee for the Society for Promoting the Return of Women as Poor Law Guardians.

---

Literature, Journalism and Publishing

# Helen Cresswell

1934 – 2005

Children's author

---

**Helen Cresswell** (11 July 1934 – 26 September 2005) was a children's author. She made her name with *Piemakers* in 1967 followed by *The Night Watchmen* in 1969, *Up the Pier* in 1971 and *The Bongleweed* in 1973. She wrote for children's television, particularly *Jackanory*, at the same time as for publication, as with her *Lizzy Dripping* series (filmed around her home) and *The Bagthorpe Saga* starting in the 1970s. She said of her work 'Whatever the outward settings of my stories, the adventures they chart are essentially inner ones', and she never plotted her books but just wrote them and followed the particular road they led her. Cresswell also adapted the work of other authors, including E.E. Nesbit's *Five Children And It.*

---

Literature, Journalism and Publishing

# Anne Grant

1755 – 1838

Poet and author

**Anne Grant** (21 February 1755 – 7 November 1838) was a poet and author. Glasgow-born, she grew up around Albany in New York where her military officer father was stationed. Returning to the Highlands in 1768, she met and married an army chaplain, James Grant, in Fort Augustus. They settled in the parish of Laggan where they had twelve children, eight of whom survived to adulthood. In 1801 James died, leaving Anne without an income, so she collected verses she had written over the years and was able to publish these poems in 1803. *Letters from the mountains* based on life in the Highlands was published in 1807 and her major work *Memoirs of an American Lady*, based on her early life, was published the following year.

# Constance Holme

1880 – 1955

Novelist and short-story writer

---

**Constance Holme** (7 October 1880 – 17 June 1955) was a novelist and short-story writer. Born in the old county of Westmorland with a father who was a land agent and deputy lord lieutenant for the county, she spend all but a few years in the hilly landscape that provided the setting for all her work. She married a local land agent Frederick Punchard and her novels explore the relationships between landowners, tenant farms and land agents. She achieved success with *Crump Folk Going Home* in 1913, set in the Milnthorpe area, and then in a series of works concentrating on characters from a more modest social class, and their hard lives, including *The Splendid Fairing* in 1919, *The Trumpet in the Dust* in 1921 and *The Things which Belong* in 1925.

# Winifred Holtby

1898 – 1935

Novelist and feminist reformer

---

**Winifred Holtby** (23 June 1898 – 29 September 1935) was a novelist and feminist reformer. After serving in the Women's Army Auxiliary Corps in 1918 she returned to studies at Somerville College, Oxford where she met and became lifelong friends with writer Vera Brittain. Socialists and pacifists, they lived together in the same household after Brittain's marriage, Holtby writing for the feminist journal *Time and Tide* as well as a string of novels focussed on independence and social and political problems, including *Anderby World* in 1923, *The Crowded Street* in 1924, *The Land of Green Ginger* in 1927 and her final novel *South Riding*, published posthumously in 1936. In 1940 Brittain published *Testament of Friendship: the story of Winifred Holtby*.

---

Literature, Journalism and Publishing

# Evelyn Irons
1900 – 2000
Journalist

---

**Evelyn Irons** (17 June 1900 – 3 April 2000) was a journalist. Initially the fashion correspondent and then women's page editor from 1931 for the *Daily Mail* Irons interviewed Radclyffe Hall, who became good friends with her and partner Olive Rinder. She then interviewed and fell in love with Vita Sackville-West. Rinder fell in love with Sackville-West too and Irons ended both relationships. She joined the *Evening Standard*, entered Germany with the Première Armée Française in 1945 as the only accredited British correspondent and was probably the first correspondent to reach Hitler's Eagle's Nest summer retreat at Berchtesgaden. She became the first woman to win France's Croix de Guerre and also broke the news embargo on the Guatemalan revolution.

# Naomi Lewis
1911 – 2009
Poet and literary critic

**Naomi Lewis** (3 September 1911 – 5 July 2009) was a poet and literary critic noted for her translations of children's books, most especially Hans Christian Andersen. Inspired to write at an early age, she taught poetry appreciation and creative writing for forty years. Winning a *New Statesman* literary competition led her to be invited to review children's books, where she became a pioneer in her field, writing many articles for newspapers and periodicals including *The New York Times* and *The Listener*. She was particularly fond of her collection of poems *Mardi Gras Cat*, described as 'absolutely magical' by A.N. Wilson. She lived in the same flat in Red Lion Square from 1935 to 2007, which became a refuge for stray cats and injured pigeons.

Literature, Journalism and Publishing

# Anne Lister
## 1791 – 1840
### Diarist and traveller

**Anne Lister** (3 April 1791 – 22 September 1840) was a diarist and traveller. She began her diaries at the age of 15 at school recording her first lesbian experiences. Dressed in black, muscular in style, Lister lived with her uncle and aunt at Shibden Hall from 1815 and eventually inherited the estate. From the 1820s she travelled in Europe, spending three years in Paris and climbing mountains in the Pyrenees. During Lister's last travels with partner Ann Walker she died from insect poisoning on the Black Sea. Her diaries, 4 million words spread over 27 volumes, detailing her life, loves and travels – about a sixth of which are in a cipher of Greek and algebra – were not published in her lifetime.

# Jane Loudon
## 1807 – 1858
### Writer on botany and magazine editor

**Jane Loudon** (19 August 1807 – 13 July 1858) was a writer on botany and pioneer of science fiction. She began a career in writing after the death of her father. In 1827 *The Mummy! A Tale of the Twenty-Second Century* was published anonymously in three volumes. Inspired by French discoveries in Egypt and Mary Shelley's *Frankenstein*, her novel predicted a mowing device, telegraph and type of internet. Reviewed favourably by John Claudius Loudon they met and were married the same year. She popularised horticulture, botany and natural history in books including *Instructions in Gardening for Ladies* in 1840 and *The First Book of Botany for Schools and Young Persons* in 1841. From 1849 to 1851 she edited the *Ladies' Companion at Home and Abroad*.

Literature, Journalism and Publishing

# Mary Norton

1903 – 1992

Children's author

**Mary Norton** (10 December 1903 – 29 August 1992) was a children's author. Marriage took her to the United States where she wrote her first children's book *The Magic Bed-Knob, or, How to Become a Witch in Ten Easy Lessons*, published in 1943. Two years later came the sequel *Bonfires and Broomsticks*. The two books were combined into *Bed-Knob and Broomstick* in 1957, becoming the Disney film *Bed Knobs and Broomsticks* in 1971. Having returned to England *The Borrowers* was published in 1952, the outstanding children's book of the year. The story of the adventures of tiny people living under the floorboards and living off the 'human beans' was followed up in a number of sequels. Norton used her childhood home as the setting for *The Borrowers*.

# Jean Rook

1931 – 1991

Journalist

---

**Jean Rook** (13 November 1931 – 5 September 1991) was a journalist known as *The First Lady of Fleet Street*. She began her career in Sheffield and Leeds, where she was Fashion Editor of the *Yorkshire Post*. After a move to London she was invited in 1964 to become Fashion Editor for *The Sun*. She moved to the *Daily Sketch* and became Woman's Editor as it merged with the *Daily Mail*. In 1972 she was poached by rival *Daily Express* to become Woman's Editor. Her journalism in a weekly column was characterised by a down-to-earth approach, her personality by her gold jewellery. A fervent supporter of Margaret Thatcher, she interviewed her nine times. Rook was the highest-paid woman in Fleet Street, and inspired the Glenda Slagg column in *Private Eye*.

---

Literature, Journalism and Publishing

# Anna Sewell

1820 – 1878

Author

**Anna Sewell** (30 March 1820 – 25 April 1878) was an author. Her mother Mary Sewell was an author of children's books. At the age of fourteen Anna slipped when running home from school in the rain and injured her ankles. Left unable to stand without a crutch or walk for any length of time, she learned to ride and use horse-drawn carriages. Her only published book was *Black Beauty*, dictated to her mother or written on scraps of paper and transcribed by her mother between 1871 and 1877 when her health was declining. It was sold to her mother's publishers Jarrold & Sons for £40. Now a children's classic, its 'special aim being to induce kindness, sympathy, and an understanding treatment of horses'. Anna died five months after publication.

# Sarah Smith
## 1832 – 1911
### Novelist and short-story writer

**Sarah Smith** (27 July 1832 – 8 October 1911) was a novelist and short-story writer. She wrote under the pseudonym, Hesba Stretton (from the first letter of the siblings names – Hannah, Elizabeth, Sarah, Benjamin and Anna, and All Stretton where Anna had property). Smith became well-known through *Jessica's First Prayer* in 1866, published in *Sunday at Home*, about a homeless child neglected by her drunken actress mother. It sold nearly 2 million copies and was translated into fifteen languages. She became the main writer for the Religious Tract Society, tackling social issues in books for children such as *Alone in London* and *Pilgrim Street*. She co-founded the London Society for the Prevention of Cruelty to Children in 1884.

Literature, Journalism and Publishing

# Anna Waring

1823 – 1910

Poet

**Anna Waring** (19 April 1823 – 10 May 1910) was a Welsh poet and hymn-writer. Born into a Quaker family she later became an Anglican and was baptised in 1842, settling in Bristol. In 1850 she published *Hymns and Meditations* with further hymns from *Additional Hymns* in 1858 integrated into later editions. Her hymns, reserved and reflective, were often reprinted in hymnbooks and anthologies, and her best known are 'Go not far from me, O my strength', 'In heavenly love abiding', 'My hear is resting, O my God' and 'Father, I know that all my life', which was played at Waring's own funeral. She was a supporter of the Discharged Prisoners' Aid Society, and visited Bridewell Prison in London and Horfield in Bristol for many years.

# Alice Ayres
1859 – 1885
Nursemaid and heroine

**Alice Ayres** (12 September 1859 – 26 April 1885) was a nursemaid who lived with the family of her brother-in-law above an oil and paint shop in Southwark. In the early hours of 24 April 1885 a fire broke out in the shop blocking the family's escape through the house. Alice ignored pleas to save herself first, dropped a feather mattress out the window and fetched in turn the three girls, aged five, four and three and dropped them from the window and they were caught. The eldest two suffered minor injuries, but the three year old died from her severe burns. Alice missed the mattress and fractured her spine and she died two days later. She is commemorated in the cloister of memorial tablets for heroic individuals in the Postman's Park in the City of London.

Medicine

# Lady Alicia Blackwood
## 1818 – 1913
Nurse and philanthropist

**Lady Alicia Blackwood** (29 November 1818 – 30 July 1913) was a nurse and philanthropist closely associated with the Crimean War. She and her husband James Blackwood were moved by the war in Crimea, and she organised a volunteer party to travel to Scutari. These experiences were recorded in a journal that became *A narrative of personal experiences and impressions during a residence on the Bosphorus throughout the Crimean War*, published in 1881. Her husband became a military chaplain and Florence Nightingale tasked Lady Alicia with sheltering women in the basements of the barrack hospital at Scutari. She then set up a women's hospital with supplies from England and charitable gifts and later a small school.

# Helen Chambers

1879 – 1935

Pathologist and cancer research worker

**Helen Chambers** (18 July 1879 – 21 July 1935) was a pathologist and cancer research expert. She studied at the London Royal Free Hospital School of Medicine for Women, becoming a lecturer there as well as being a clinical pathologist at the Royal Free Hospital, and obtained her Doctor of Medicine in Pathology in 1908. Consultant pathologist at Endell Street Military Hospital during the war, she introduced the new Bipp antiseptic treatment. Her research speciality was radium at Middlesex Hospital before and after the war. Focussing on radiotherapy for treating cancer of the cervix, she campaigned for a centre for treating women's cancers, and the Marie Curie Hospital opened in 1929. Her own life was cut short by breast cancer.

# Eleanor Davies-Colley

1874 – 1934

Surgeon and a founder of the South London
Hospital for Women and Children

**Eleanor Davies-Colley** (21 August 1874 – 10
December 1934) was a surgeon and a founder of
the South London Hospital for Women and
Children. The daughter of a surgeon at Guys
Hospital, she worked with deprived children in
London's East End before studying medicine at the
London School of Medicine for Women, where she
obtained her MB in 1907 and became house
surgeon at the New Hospital for Women founded
by Elizabeth Garrett Anderson. After obtaining her
MD in 1910 she became the first woman to obtain
the fellowship of the Royal College of Surgeons.
Davies-Colley raised funds with partner Maud
Chadburn for what became the South London
Hospital for Women and Children, opening in
Clapham a purpose-built hospital in 1916 where
she worked to her death.

Medicine

# Elizabeth Haldane

1862 – 1937

Author, philosopher and nursing administrator

**Elizabeth Haldane** (27 May 1862 – 24 December 1937) was an author, philosopher and nursing administrator. Self-taught, she translated Hegel's *The History of Philosophy* in 1892 with Frances Simson and wrote a *Life of Descartes* in 1903 as well as biographies on George Eliot and Elizabeth Gaskell. Haldane took nursing courses, became a manager at the Edinburgh Royal Infirmary and was involved in establishing the Voluntary Aid Detachment (VAD) from 1908. During the war she was vice-chair of the territorial nursing service and was made Companion of Honour in 1918 in recognition of her war work. Haldane became the first woman trustee of the Carnegie United Kingdom Trust in 1913, and the first female Justice of the Peace in Scotland in 1920.

# Dame Mary Scharlieb

1845 – 1930

Gynaecologist

**Dame Mary Scharlieb** (18 June 1845 – 21 November 1930) was a gynaecologist. After marrying William Scharlieb in 1865 they lived in India where she qualified as a midwife at Madras Medical College. Returning to England she trained at Elizabeth Garret Anderson's London School of Medicine for Women, obtaining a gold medal for obstetrics. She left for India again in 1883 and helped found the Royal Victoria Hospital for Caste and Gosha women. Scharlieb took her MD degree on her return to England in 1888, then was surgeon at the New Hospital for Women from 1892 to 1903 and gynaecologist at the Royal Free Hospital in 1902, alongside establishing a private practice. She championed professional careers for women and was widely respected in her field.

# Alexandra ('Mona') Chalmers Watson
## 1872 – 1936
### Medical practitioner and head of the Women's Army Auxiliary Corps

**Alexander ('Mona') Chalmers Watson** (31 May 1872 – 7 August 1936) was a medical practitioner and head of the Women's Army Auxiliary Corps. The first woman to receive an MD from the University of Edinburgh in 1898, Chalmers Watson ran a private practice with her husband. Alongside this she helped found the Elsie Inglis Hospital, became president of both the Scottish Women's Medical Association and British Women's Medical Federation and assisted her husband edit the *Encyclopedia medica* from 1899 to 1910. During the war she was appointed Chief Controller of the Women's Army Auxiliary Corps, for which she recruited over 40,000 women. From 1923 she and her husband were pioneers in improving the quality of milk at their farm in the East Lothian.

Medicine

# Helena Wright

1887 – 1982

Family planning practitioner and sex therapist

---

**Helena Wright** (17 September 1887 – 21 March 1982) was a pioneering figure in the fields of birth control and family planning. She studied medicine at the London Royal Free School for Medicine for Women and undertook missionary work in China during the 1920s, specialising in gynaecology. On her return to London Margery Rice offered Helena the role of Chief Medical Officer at the Women's Centre in North Kensington, where she worked for thirty years and trained nurses and medical students in birth control and sex education. She was also instrumental in the setting up of the National Birth Control Association, and wrote a successful book *The Sex Factor in Marriage.*

# Grace ('Gracie') Cole
1924 – 2006
Trumpeter

**Grace ('Gracie') Cole** (8 September 1924 – 28 December 2006) was a trumpeter who broke into the previously all-male preserve of brass and dance bands during the 1930s and 1940s. Her father was a miner and musician who played cornet in colliery bands in Yorkshire. He taught her to play the cornet when she was twelve years old and was soon playing in brass bands and made her first broadcast in 1939 for *Children's Hour*. After switching to being a dance band trumpeter she joined the Ivy Benson Band in 1945 as lead trumpet and soloist, touring with them for five years, before forming her own all-female band. She married the trombonist Bill Geldard in 1951 and after the birth of their daughters they encouraged the development of local brass bands.

Music

# Marion Scott

1877 – 1953

Musicologist

**Marion Scott** (16 July 1877 – 24 December 1953) was a musicologist. Trained as a violinist at the Royal College of Music, she founded the Marion Scott Quartet in 1908 to promote contemporary British music. She also was one of the founders of the Society of Women Musicians in 1911, serving as its president from 1915 to 1916. From 1919 her writing about music featured in leading music magazines. She formed a strong friendship with the poet and composer Ivor Gurney, and enabled to get his poetry from the war front, *Severn and Somme*, published in 1917. She helped him after his breakdown, and published the first three volumes of his songs in 1938 and 1952. Scott also became the leading authority on Haydn and published a classic book on Beethoven.

# Phyllis Tate
1911 – 1987

Composer

**Phyllis Tate** (6 April 1911 – 29 May 1987) was a composer. After studying at the Royal Academy of Music from 1928 to 1932 she had several pieces premiered before the war, including a cello concerto in 1934. She later destroyed all her works before 1944, the year she was commissioned by the BBC and composed first a concerto for alto saxophone and strings, then a chamber cantata *Nocturne for Four Voices* in 1945, and a sonata for clarinet and cello in 1947. She believed that music should entertain and give pleasure, and she loved creating unusual sounds and textures. In the 1950s she focussed increasingly on choral music, including a cantata to Tennyson's poem *The Lady of Shallott* in 1956 and an opera *The Lodger* based on the Jack the Ripper story.

Music

# Dame Maeve Fort
1940 – 2008
Diplomat

**Dame Maeve Fort** (19 November 1940 – 18 September 2008) rose to become the highest ranking female British diplomat. She joined the Foreign Office in 1962. In 1978 during a posting to New York she began to specialise in African affairs, being part of the group working towards Namibian independence. In 1989 she became Ambassador to Mozambique and was involved in negotiations to bring civil war to an end. Her next posting in Lebanon from 1992 was also dangerous, even after the end of the civil war the year before, and she was accompanied there by six bodyguards. In 1996 she was appointed High Commissioner to South Africa, where she had a close working relationship with Nelson Mandela.

# Olive Morris

1952 – 1979

Political activist

**Olive Morris** (26 June 1952 – 12 July 1979) was a political activist. Born in Jamaica her family moved to Lavender Hill in South London when she was nine years old. Against a background of racism in Britain in the early 1970s she was a founding member of the Brixton Black Women's Group. She and Liz Obi squatted at 122 Railton Road in 1973, helping its transformation into a pioneering black community bookshop. In 1978, after studying economics and social sciences at Manchester University, Morris founded with others the Organization of Women of African and Asian Descent (OWAAD) and returning to Brixton, involved herself in a campaign to scrap 'sus' laws. She died aged twenty-seven after being diagnosed with non-Hodgkin's lymphoma. She features on the £1 Brixton pound.

Politics, Government and Diplomacy

# Catherine Booth

1829 – 1890

Evangelist and co-founder of the Salvation Army

---

**Catherine Booth** (17 January 1829 – 4 October 1890) was an evangelist and co-founder of the Salvation Army. By the time she was twelve it was said she had read the bible eight times. In 1851 she met William Booth, a lay preacher; they were married in 1855 and had eight children together. She wrote a pamphlet in 1859, later revised and published as *The Female Ministry, or, Women's right to Preach* in 1870. She and the family accompanied William as he worked as an evangelist first for the Methodist New Connexion and then independently until 1865 when they established the East London Christian Mission. She raised funds for the Mission, helping it grow to seventy-two mission stations by 1879 when it became the Salvation Army.

---

# Annie Taylor
1855 – 1922
Traveller and missionary

**Annie Taylor** (17 October 1855 – 9 September 1922) was a traveller and Evangelical missionary in China, becoming the first Western woman known to have visited Tibet. A converted Evangelical Christian, she joined the China Inland Mission in 1884 and was posted to Lanzhou, close to the border with Tibet, for two years. Ill health forced her to leave China in 1888 but while studying the Tibetan language in a Sikkim monastery she met a young Tibetan named Pontso, with whom she returned to China in 1891. They planned to ride through Tibet to the forbidden city of Lhasa, but after travelling 1,300 miles were stopped at the beginning of 1893 just days away from Lhasa and were led out of China. She returned in 1894 and again in 1904.

Religion and Belief

# Janet Arnold

1932 – 1998

Costume historian

---

**Janet Arnold** (6 October 1932 – 2 November 1998) was a specialist in historical costume, noted for the three volumes of *Patterns of Fashion (vol 1: 1660 -1860), (vol 2: 1860-1940) and (vol 3: 1560-1620).* After studying design in dress and obtaining experience in London couture houses, she became a lecturer on fashion, dressmaking and theatre design. An avid theatre-goer, her research also extended into working in holidays in the wardrobes at the Theatre Royal in Bristol and Mermaid Theatre in London. She travelled extensively to photograph surviving garments. *Patterns of Fashion* combined this research with her drawings and accurate scale patterns. These books led to her advice being sought by museum curators and theatre designers.

---

Scholarship and Research

# Hertha Ayrton

1854 – 1923

Electrical engineer and suffragist

---

**Sarah** (called **Hertha**) **Ayrton** (28 April 1854 – 23 August 1923) was an electrical engineer and suffragist. After studying Mathematics at Cambridge she went in 1884 to evening classes on electricity run by the electrical engineer William Ayrton; they married the following year. She discovered that electric arcs lights flickered and hissed due to oxygen coming into contact with carbon rods, and published her analysis in *The Electrician* from 1895, and later in her book *The Electric Arc* in 1902. Interests in vortices in water and air led to the development of the Ayrton fan, or flapper, used in the trenches during the Great War to dispel poison gas. She was the first woman to win a Royal Society prize, the Hughes Medal in 1906.

---

Scholarship and Research

# Nicolete Gray

1911 – 1997

Historian of lettering, letter carver and art critic

---

**Nicolete Gray** (20 July 1911 – 8 June 1997) was a historian of lettering, letter carver and art critic. She studied history at Lady Margaret Hall, Oxford, then travelled through Italy studying medieval inscriptions on a scholarship to the British School at Rome. She began writing art criticism for *Art and Letters* and through a friendship she formed with Helen Sutherland developed an interest in contemporary art, and she went on to put on the Abstract and Concrete exhibition in 1936. In 1938 she published *XIXth Century Ornamented Types and Titles*, from specimen type books arranged chronologically by each founder in St Bride Printing Library, followed many years later with *A History of Lettering*. She married art historian Basil Gray in 1933.

---

# Dame Elizabeth Hill

1900 – 1996

Russian and Slavonic scholar

**Dame Elizabeth Hill** (24 October 1900 – 17 December 1996) was a Russian and Slavonic scholar. The daughter of a British father and Russian mother, the family left Russia in 1917 and Elizabeth completed her degree in Russian in London in 1924 and her PhD by 1931. She translated letters written by Dostoyevsky to his wife and Lenin. She became a lecturer in Slavonic at the University of Cambridge in 1936, promoted to Professor in 1948 and building a reputation with her teaching of the Russian language. During the Second World War she was employed by the Ministry of Information as a Slavonic specialist, setting up Russian language courses for the War Office.

Scholarship and Research

# Mary Impey, Lady Impey
## 1749 – 1818
### Natural historian and patron of the arts

**Mary Impey, Lady Impey** (2 March 1749 – 20 February 1818) was a natural historian and patron of the arts. In 1768 she married the barrister Elijah Impey and in 1873 he was made chief justice in Bengal. They travelled to India in 1774 and settled in Fort William, where she started collecting native birds, animals and native plants in the gardens of their mansion, making extensive notes about their behaviour and habitat. From 1777 to 1782 she commissioned local artists Sheikh Zain al-Din, Bhavani Das and Ram Das to make large drawings of her collection using a Mughal technique of layering brilliant colours. The bird drawings were painted life-size from life in their natural surroundings.

# Diana Kirkbride

1915 – 1997

Archaeologist

**Diana Kirkbride** (22 October 1915 – 13 August 1997)
was a specialist in Palestinian and Mesopotamian
archaeology. After reading Egyptology at
University College, London in the late 1940s she
studied at the Institute of Archaelogy in London
under the direction of Dame Kathleen Kenyon and
Sir Max Mallowan. In 1953 she was employed by
Gerald Lankester Harding, director of antiquities for
Jordan, who engaged her on the excavation and
restoration of a ruined temple in Jerash, and then
on the excavation at Beidha, revealing a Natufian
settlement from around 10,000 BC, and in so
changing perspectives on Near Eastern prehistoric
archaeology. She later worked in Lebanon and
Iraq, and was married to the Danish paleobotanist
Hans Helbaek.

Scholarship and Research

# Damaris, Lady Masham

1658 – 1708

Philosopher and theological writer

**Damaris, Lady Masham** (18 January 1658 – 20 April 1708) was a philosopher and theological writer. Brought up in a family where enquiry and learning were encouraged, she met the philosopher John Locke in 1682 and they became close friends, and he taught her philosophy and divinity. She married Sir Francis Masham in 1685 and they lived at Otes in Essex where Locke was first a frequent visitor, then invited to live with them from 1691 until his death in 1704. Masham and Locke spent most of their time together exchanging philosophical ideas. In 1696 she published an essay on morality *A Discourse Concerning the Love of God* and in 1705 *Occasional thoughts in reference to a vertuous or Christian Life*, both anonymously.

# Rosalind Moss

1890 – 1990

Egyptologist and bibliographer

**Rosalind Moss** (21 September 1890 – 22 April 1990) was an Egyptologist and bibliographer, most well known for her work published as *The Topographical Bibliography of Ancient Egyptian Hieroglyphic Texts, Reliefs and Paintings*. She took up Egyptology under Professor Francis Griffith, who realised in her an ideal collaborator for his bibliography of ancient Egyptian monuments because of her organisational skill and energy. The volumes of the bibliography were published steadily onwards from 1927 up to the seventh volume in 1951. After Griffith died their library became the Griffith Institute in 1939, where she worked until she retired in 1970. She died just short of her 100th birthday.

Scholarship and Research

# Anna Swanwick

1813 – 1899

Translator, writer and social reformer

**Anna Swanwick** (22 June 1813 – 2 November 1899) was a translator and social reformer. After studying German and Greek in Berlin she translated German and Greek dramatists, including Goethe's *Faust* in 1850 and 1878 and the *Trilogy* of Aeschylus. Interested in the education of women, she supported both Queen's College from 1848 and Bedford College from 1850, assisted funding of Girton College, Cambridge and Somerville Hall, Oxford and was joint trustee of the Pfeiffer bequest for women's higher education. Swanwick was the first elected woman member of the Royal Institution in 1858, supported the call for a woman's right to vote in 1865 and was friends with many leading figures of the day, including Carlyle, Faraday, Tennyson and Browning.

Scholarship and Research

# Philippa Fawcett

1868 – 1948

Mathematician and civil servant

**Philippa Fawcett** (4 April 1868 – 10 June 1948) was a mathematician and educationalist. The only daughter of suffragist leader Millicent Garrett Fawcett and politician Henry Fawcett, she was educated at Newnham College, Cambridge, co-founded by her mother. In 1890 her mathematical tripos result was 13% higher than the second best score of the best male student, 'the senior wrangler'. A scholarship at Newnham on fluid dynamics was followed by being college lecturer for ten years, before she left to train teachers in South Africa. In 1905 she took charge of higher education at the London county council, setting up new secondary schools and particularly focussing on teacher training.

Science

# Dame Honor Fell
1900 – 1986
Cell biologist

**Dame Honor Fell** (22 May 1900 – 22 April 1986) was a cell biologist. After studying Zoology at Edinburgh University she began working for Thomas Strangeways at the Cambridge Research Hospital until the latter died in 1926. By 1929 Fell was Director of the renamed Strangeways Research Laboratory; over the next forty-one years the laboratory became a world renowned centre for studies in cell biology and particularly in vitro techniques. She focussed on organ and tissue culture including work on the breakdown of tissue by lysosomal enzymes, the histogenesis of bone and cartilage and the importance of synovial tissue in the breakdown of bone and cartilage, along with the action of vitamin A on bone, skin and membranes.

# Catherine Raisin

1855 – 1945

Geologist and educationalist

**Catherine Raisin** (24 April 1855 – 12 July 1945) was a geologist and educationalist. She studied Geology and Zoology at University College, London the year after degrees were opened up to women and was the first woman to study Geology there, becoming the top Geology graduate in 1884. After joining Bedford College for Women in 1886 she became head of the Geology department in 1890, and later also the Botany and Geography departments. The first woman to receive the Lyell Fund award by the Geological Society of London in 1893, Raisin's interests were mainly in microscopic petrology and mineralogy, publishing twenty-four papers between 1887 and 1905. She additionally founded in 1880 the Somerville Club, a discussion group for women with over 1,000 members.

Science

# Charlotte Scott

1858 – 1931

Mathematician

---

**Charlotte Scott** (8 June 1858 – 10 November 1931) was a mathematician. She studied at Girton College, Cambridge from 1876 and in 1880, allowed to take the Tripos Exam, she was eighth, but due to her gender 'eighth wrangler' went to a male student. The following year Cambridge University voted to rank women with men. In 1885 Bryn Mawr College, Pennsylvania offered her a position as Associate Professor. In 1891 she was the first woman to join the New York Mathematical Society, co-edited the *American Journal of Mathematics* and in 1905 to 1906 was Vice-President of the American Mathematical Society. Her lectures on projective geometry were published in *An Introductory Account of Certain Modern Ideas and Methods in Plane Analytical Geometry* in 1894.

# Louisa Baring, Lady Ashburton
1827 – 1903
Art collector and philanthropist

**Louisa Baring, Lady Ashburton** (5 March 1827 – 2 February 1903) was an art collector and philanthropist. She married the fifty-nine year old Bingham Baring in 1858 and had a daughter together. When he died in 1864 she began a collection of paintings, drawings and sculptures, including works by Rubens, Mantegna and Titian as well as works by contemporary artists such as Rossetti, Lear and Watts. She maintained correspondences with many well-known figures of the day including Carlyle, Ruskin, Lear, Browning, Nightingale, Landseer and Lady Trevelyan. In her later years she supported numerous causes: including a seaman's mission, the Metropolitan Tabernacle and the Islington and Holy Mission Fund, Bethnal Green.

# Florence Barrow

1876 – 1964

Relief worker and promoter of improving housing

**Florence Barrow** (27 January 1876 – 3 March 1964) was a relief worker and promoter of improved housing. The only daughter of a Quaker businessman and Mayor of Birmingham her 'outward appearance (she was only four feet six inches tall) gave little indication of the power within'. In 1916 she did relief work in western Russia, setting up nurseries for abandoned children, pharmacies, workshops and feeding centres. In 1919 she distributed food relief in Germany crippled by the Great War. In 1924 she co-founded the Birmingham Conference on Politics, Economics and Citizenship (COPEC) and focussed on slum clearance and inner city housing regeneration over a period of thirty-seven years, a period punctuated as a secret agent in Nazi Germany and Austria.

# Helen Blackburn

1842 – 1903

Campaigner for women's rights

**Helen Blackburn** (25 May 1842 – 11 January 1903) was a campaigner for women's rights. After moving from native Ireland to London in 1859 she became involved in suffrage and women's employment causes through Jessie Boucherett at the Langham Place Group. She became successively secretary at the National Society of Women's Suffrage from 1874 to 1880 and the Bristol and West of England Society for Women's Suffrage from 1880 to 1895. She was editor and joint editor with Boucherett of the *Englishwoman's Review,* publishing together *The Condition of Working Women and the Factory Acts* in 1896. In 1902 she finished *Women's Suffrage: a record of the women's suffrage movement in the British Isles* and *Women under the Factory Act* in 1903 with Nora Vynne.

# Nicky Chapman, Baroness Chapman

1961 – 2009

Disability campaigner

**Nicky Chapman, Baroness Chapman** (3 August 1961 – 3 September 2009) was a disability campaigner. Born with Osteogenesis Imperfecta (brittle bone disease) she lived to the age of forty-eight when she was only expected to live hours. She used an electric wheelchair, was less than three feet tall, constantly suffered fractures and was in acute pain. She campaigned for independent living and access to public buildings. The first person with a congenital disability to enter the House of Lords in 2004, she critiqued the Mental Capacity Bill in 2005 and forced legislation change with taxi drivers duty bound to transport wheelchair passengers. The Nicky Chapman Award since 2011 has encouraged disabled people to enter the housing sector.

# Emily Davies

1830 – 1921

Suffragist and promoter of
higher education for women

---

**Emily Davies** (22 April 1830 – 13 July 1921) was a suffragist and promoter of higher education for women. In 1862 she wrote a paper *Medicine as a profession for women* and began writing for the *English Woman's Journal* which she also edited in 1863. In 1865 she was a founder member of the ladies' debating group, the Kensington Society and helped obtain 1,500 female signatories for a petition in favour of women's suffrage, presented to the House of Commons in 1866. That year she published her book *The Higher Education of Women* and co-formed the committee wanting to build a college for women in Cambridge. Founded in 1869 Girtin College moved to the outskirts of Cambridge in 1873 and became the first college founded to educate women in England.

Social Welfare and Reform

# Margaret Llewelyn Davies
## 1861 – 1944
### Campaigner for women's causes

**Margaret Llewelyn Davies** (16 October 1861 – 28 May 1944) was a campaigner for women's issues. The daughter of an active Christian Socialist, she became General Secretary of the Women's Co-operative Guild in 1889 and ran it with her friend Lillian Harris in Kirkby Lonsdale for thirty-two years. The Guild encouraged women to organise themselves into peaceful co-operative societies to help themselves change the things that impacted upon their lives. Under Davies the Guild grew from fifty-one branches and 1,700 members to 1,038 branches and 52,000 members. The Guild advocated divorce law reform, suffrage for women and in 1915 she published *Maternity: Letters from Working Women*, detailing the experiences of childbirth and child-rearing from 400 of the Guild's members.

Social Welfare and Reform

# Princess Sophia Duleep Singh

1876 – 1948

Suffragette

**Princess Sophia Duleep Singh** (8 August 1876 – 22 August 1948) was a suffragette. Maharaja Duleep Singh was her father and Queen Victoria her godmother, thanks to whom she lived in a grace and favour apartment in Hampton Court. She campaigned for votes for women with the Women's Social and Political Union; helped fundraise and was a seller of *The Suffragette* and was part of the 'Black Friday' group who went to the House of Commons in 1909 seeking a meeting with the Prime Minister. For the Women's Tax Resistance League (WTRL), she refused to pay licence fees for her dogs and carriage, leading to the seizing of her assets that were then bought back for her by members of the WTRL. Duleep Singh was also a Red Cross nurse during the Great War.

Social Welfare and Reform

# Elizabeth Elmy
## 1833 – 1918
### Campaigner for women's rights

**Elizabeth Elmy** (30 November 1833 – 12 March 1918) was a campaigner for women's rights. Orphaned by the age of fourteen, she took over a girls' school in Boothstown and moved it to Congleton in Cheshire. In 1865 Elmy founded the Manchester Board of Schoolmistresses and became honorary secretary of the Manchester Society for Women's Suffrage. In 1867 she became honorary secretary to the Married Women's Property Committee. In 1871 she formed with Josephine Butler and others the Committee for Amending the Law in Points Injurious to Women and the Vigilance Association for the Defence of Personal Rights. She was a founding member of the Women's Franchise League in 1889 and in 1892 established the Women's Emancipation League.

Social Welfare and Reform

# Ethel Fenwick

1857 – 1947

Leader of the campaign for
state registration of nurses

**Ethel Fenwick** (26 January 1857 – 13 March 1947) was the leader of the campaign for the state registration of nurses. She trained as a nurse and worked as a matron at St Bartholomew's Hospital in London before she married the physician Bedford Fenwick in 1887. She founded the British Nurses' Association that year to lobby for the state registration of trained nurses. She took over the *Nursing Record* journal in 1893 and was instrumental in founding the International Council of Nurses in 1899. In 1902 Ethel and her husband drafted the first bill for state registration but, in spite of select committee approval, opposition meant the Registration Act was only passed in 1919. Fenwick appeared as 'Nurse No. 1' in the register.

Social Welfare and Reform

# Mary Gawthorpe

1881 – 1973

Suffragist and socialist

---

**Mary Gawthorpe** (12 January 1881 – 12 March 1973) was a suffragist and socialist. After qualifying as a teacher Mary joined first the National Union of Women's Suffrage Societies in 1905 but was drawn to the militants of the Women's Social and Political Union (WSPU). Mary became involved in local politics as vice-president of the Leeds branch of the Independent Labour Party in 1906. She went to prison for the suffrage cause that year, and in subsequent jailings went on hunger strike. She also suffered assaults in 1909 after heckling Churchill on Polling Day in January 1910. In 1911 she co-founded *The Freewoman*, a radical periodical. She emigrated to the United States in 1916, and wrote about her early life in *Up Hill to Holloway* in 1962.

---

Social Welfare and Reform

# Eva Hubback
## 1886 – 1949
### Social reformer and feminist

**Eva Hubback** (13 April 1886 – 15 July 1949) was a social reformer and feminist. After obtaining a first in Economics at Newnham College, Cambridge, she worked with the suffragists and became parliamentary secretary and later president of the National Union for Equal Citizenship, campaigning for reforms of laws concerning women and children. In 1927 she became Principal of Morley College, making it a well known centre for music, theatre, ballet and art. She established the Townswomen's Guild in 1930 and was a co-founder of the Association for Education in Citizenship in 1934. Her interest in population issues came from her work with the Eugenics Society and Family Planning Association and she published *Population of Britain* in 1947.

Social Welfare and Reform

# Louisa Hubbard

1836 – 1906

## Promoter of employment and educational opportunities for women

**Louisa Hubbard** (8 March 1836 – 25 November 1906) was a promoter of employment and educational opportunities for women. Born into a wealthy merchant family, she used her wealth to fund women's causes and campaigns. She published *Work for Ladies in Elementary Schools* in 1872 and in 1873 established Otter College in Chichester as a teacher training college for women. She pioneered the provision of information about opportunities open to women in *A Guide to All Institutions for the Benefit of Women* from 1869 to 1878 and edited two publications *The Handbook of Women's Work* and the *Women's Gazette* in 1875. She supported numerous other causes including The Ladies' Dwellings Company, Gentlewomen's Employment Club and Women's Emigration Society.

Social Welfare and Reform

# Eglantyne Jebb

1876 – 1928

Philanthropist

**Eglantyne Jebb** (25 August 1876 – 17 December 1928) was a philanthropist who founded the Save the Children Fund. As part of the Charity Organisation Society she wrote in 1906 *Cambridge: a Brief Study in Social Questions*, outlining social problems in the city. After working in Macedonia in 1913 after the Second Balkan War she promoted the Macedonian Relief Fund. This led her and sister Dorothy to focus on the plight of millions of children starving at the end of the Great War. They launched the Fight the Famine Council, precursor to the Save the Children Fund, at the Royal Albert Hall in 1919 and set up The International Save the Children Fund in Geneva in 1920. In 1923 she drafted a Children's Charter, and, as the Declaration of Geneva, was adopted by the League of Nations in 1924.

Social Welfare and Reform

# Dame Agnes Jekyll

1861 – 1937

Philanthropist and political hostess

**Dame Agnes Jekyll** (12 October 1861 – 28 January 1937) was a philanthropist and political hostess noted for her involvement in numerous good causes. The daughter of Liberal MP and art collector William Graham, she married in 1881 Sir Herbert Jekyll, a captain in the Royal Engineers and brother of the garden designer Gertrude Jekyll. During the Great War she was chairman of the St John of Jerusalem's warehouse for hospital supplies and volunteered on ambulance service. She was a member of the East End maternity hospital committee, a magistrate sitting on the panel of Guildford children's court and chair of the visiting committee of the Borstal Institution for Girls. Her *Kitchen Essays* in housekeeping skills was published in 1922.

# Dame Grace Kimmins

1870 – 1954

Welfare reformer for disabled children

---

**Dame Grace Kimmins** (6 May 1870 – 3 March 1954) was a welfare reformer for disabled children and others with disabilities. In 1894 she founded the Guild of the Poor Brave Things and the Guild of Play to provide help for the disabled in Bermondsey. There she met her future husband, Charles Kimmins, a council inspector of education. In 1902 they set up the Chailey Heritage Craft School in Sussex, along with close friend Alice Rennie, bringing seven disabled boys from London as its first residents. It was a success and they took over a disused school and expanded services for girls after 1908, training boys in leather and woodwork and girls in sewing and needlework. After the Great War they extended services to disabled soldiers and sailors.

---

Social Welfare and Reform

# Margaret MacDonald
1870 – 1911
Socialist and feminist

**Margaret MacDonald** (20 July 1870 – 8 September 1911) was a socialist and feminist. Voluntary work she undertook early in adulthood in London drew her into socialism, inspired by speeches of trade union leader Ben Tillett and by the Fabian society's *Fabian Essays* in 1893. She met husband Ramsay MacDonald, the first future Labour Prime Minister, in 1895. In 1894 she joined the Women's Industrial Council, a group focussed on bettering the lives of female industrial workers. In 1904 she produced a series of studies on women workers. She was equally involved with the National Union of Women Workers and the Women's Labour League, and was also closely linked to improving the lives of unemployed women. She died of blood poisoning aged forty-one.

# Dame Sheila McKechnie

## 1948 – 2004

### Housing reformer and consumer rights campaigner

---

**Dame Sheila McKechnie** (3 May 1948 – 2 January 2004) was a housing reformer and consumer rights campaigner. In the 1970s she was a trade union official, and involved in the women's movement, and journal *Red Rag*. She rejuvenated Shelter from 1985 to 1995, criticising existing government housing policy focussed on home ownership and developed homelessness services. From 1995 she became director of the Consumers' Association, campaigning on stronger food standards and regulations, greater competition in the car market and reforms in financial services, especially the mis-selling of endowment mortgages. She was president of the European Union Consumer Group championing better labelling and regulation of the promotion of pharmaceutical products.

---

Social Welfare and Reform

# Dame Sarah Mair

1846 – 1941

Promoter of women's education and campaigner for women's rights

---

**Dame Sarah Mair** (23 September 1846 – 13 February 1941) was a Scottish campaigner for women's education and suffrage. She set up the Edinburgh Essay Society in 1865 (later Ladies' Edinburgh Debating Society) that met each month in the Mair family home. She remained its president for over 70 years. She championed women's suffrage and became president of the Edinburgh National Society for Women's Suffrage, and of the Scottish Federation of Women's Suffrage Societies. After 1918 when women over the age of thirty were given the vote she helped re-orientate the Society into the Society for Equal Citizenship. Mair was also instrumental in setting up St George's Training College for training women as secondary school teachers and St George's High School for Girls.

---

Social Welfare and Reform

# Emily Massingberd
1847 – 1897

Founder of the Pioneer Club and temperance
campaigner

---

**Emily Massingberd** (19 December 1847 – 28 January 1897) was the Founder of the Pioneer Club and a temperance campaigner. After her husband died in 1875 she was left with a young son and three daughters, and she turned to temperance work with the British Women's Temperance Association. She made her first speech supporting the women's suffrage movement in 1882. In 1892 she founded the Pioneer Club to provide middle-class women and particularly unmarried women with a place to socialise outside their homes. By the mid 1890s membership had risen to over 300 and double that by the end of the century. The club organised lectures, debates and discussion every Thursday evening on social, literary and political matters. It remained active to 1939.

---

Social Welfare and Reform

# Hilda Murrell
## 1906 – 1984
### Environmentalist and peace campaigner

**Hilda Murrell** (3 February 1906 – 21 March 1984) was an environmentalist and peace campaigner. She joined her family firm of rose growers, directing it from 1930 to 1970. Murrell was a founder member of the Shropshire Conservation Trust in 1962 and particularly loved the Welsh marches, as recorded in her posthumous *Nature Diaries* in 1987. She became increasingly concerned by the nuclear power industry and nuclear weapons, joining the European Nuclear Disarmament Movement in 1981 and peace campaigns and wrote a paper criticising the government white paper on radioactive waste management for the Sizewell B enquiry in 1984. She was murdered in mysterious circumstances that same year. After her death David Austin named a rose after her.

# Margaret Nevinson

1858 – 1932

Women's rights activist

---

**Margaret Nevinson** (11 January 1858 – 8 June 1932) was a women's rights activist. A school manager for twenty-five years and poor-law guardian in Hampstead from 1904, she was one of the founders of the Women's Freedom League (WFL) in 1907 as it split from the Women's Social and Political Union (WSPU) and wrote the suffrage pamphlet *A History of the Suffrage Movement: 1908-1912*. She was particularly concerned with gender-specific legislation that discriminated against married women, the theme also of her play *In the Workhouse*. After the war she became a justice of the peace and was the first woman in London to adjudicate at petty criminal sessions. She was married to the journalist Henry Woodd Nevinson, and their son was the artist Christopher.

---

# Tess Simpson

1903 – 1996

Worker for refugee scholars

**Tess Simpson** (31 July 1903 – 19 November 1996) worked for refugee scholars who fled Nazi Germany. The daughter of Lithuanian Jewish immigrants, she won a scholarship to study French and German at Leeds University from 1921 and used her languages for translator and interpreter work in Europe. Her career focussed on helping scholars fleeing Hitler's Germany after 1933 at what became known as the Society for the Protection of Science and Learning. Up to 1940 she welcomed 2,600 refugees, including Karl Popper, Ernst Gombrich and Nikolaus Pevsner, settling them into their new life in colleges and universities in Britain, the Commonwealth and the United States. She fought successfully for their release after internment under Churchill.

Social Welfare and Reform

# Louisa Stevenson

1835 – 1908

Campaigner for women's rights

**Louisa Stevenson** (15 July 1835 – 13 May 1908) was a campaigner for women's rights. She became involved with the Edinburgh Ladies' Educational Association (later Edinburgh Association for the University Education of Women), helping get Scottish universities to admit women in 1892, as well as donating funds for a woman's hall of residence, Masson Hall, opened in 1897. Stevenson was the first woman elected as a poor-law guardian in Edinburgh and set about improving the quality of nursing in city poorhouses. She was elected a member of the Edinburgh Royal Infirmary Board, the first woman to serve on a hospital board and supported women's suffrage as an executive committee member of the National Union of Women's Suffrage Societies.

Social Welfare and Reform

# Emily Sturge

## 1847 – 1892

### Campaigner for women's education and suffrage

---

**Emily Sturge** (20 April 1847 – 3 June 1892) was a campaigner for women's education and suffrage. Born into a Quaker family with five sisters involved in women's education, in 1878 she became honorary secretary of the west of England branch of the National Society for Women's Suffrage, and campaigned through the Liberal party to obtain the vote for women. She taught in a Friends' Sunday school, was involved with an elementary school for girls, and was elected to the Bristol school board in 1880. There she campaigned for 'penny dinners' free school meals, set up evening schools and promoted training and the status of women teachers, fund-raising for University College and helping establish in 1892 a day training school for women teachers.

---

# Lucy Townsend

1781 – 1847

Slavery abolitionist

---

**Lucy Townsend** (25 July 1781 – 20 April 1847) was a slavery abolitionist. She founded and became joint-secretary with Mary Lloyd of the Ladies' Society for the Relief of Negro Slaves in 1825 at her home in West Bromwich. It became the model for a network of female anti-slavery societies both in Britain and the United States. The society particularly focussed on the plight of women under slavery. Author of an anti-slavery pamphlet *To the Law and to the Testimony* in 1832, she attended the World Anti-Slavery Convention in London in 1840 but she did not put herself to be included in the group painted portrait that commemorated the event. She also campaigned for those who were deaf and mute and against cruel sports.

# Mary Townsend
1841 – 1918
Philanthropist

**Mary Townsend** (23 July 1841 – 14 June 1918) was a philanthropist and founder of the Girls' Friendly Society. Married to wealthy botanist Frederick Townsend, she was asked to undertake some rescue work for fallen women in 1873. Seeing that prevention was better than cure, she founded the society in 1875 to provide protection, love and kindness to unmarried working girls aged fourteen upwards. Arranged by parish groups, the society provided recreation rooms for girls to meet, read, sew and sing. She served as president from 1876 to 1883 and from 1891 to 1894, wrote for various society journals and saw the society grow from 10,000 members in 1876 to over 197,000 members by 1913, then cared for women war workers during the Great War.

# Mabel Tuke
1871 – 1962
Suffragette

**Mabel Tuke** (19 May 1871 – 22 November 1962) was a suffragette. Twice-previously married, she met and became friends with Emmeline Pethick-Lawrence in 1905 on a boat journey home to England from South Africa and was introduced to the Women's Social and Political Union formed by Emmeline Pankhurst. Tuke became the WSPU honorary secretary in 1906 and formed a strong bond with Emmeline and daughter Christabel. Her activities were mainly peaceful, but on 1st March 1912 Tuke was arrested and imprisoned for three weeks after throwing a stone through the window of 10 Downing Street. She and the Pankhursts remained close; living in Paris with Christabel in 1913 and running a tea-shop with them in 1925 at Juan-les-Pins on the French Riviera.

Social Welfare and Reform

# Maureen Gardner
## 1928 – 1974
### Athlete and ballet teacher

**Maureen Gardner** (12 November 1928 – 2 September 1974) was an athlete and ballet teacher. During the Second World War she contracted bronchial pneumonia and pleurisy and after she had recovered she was encouraged to take up sport to regain her strength. At the same time she was working as a ballet teacher. In 1946 she was spotted by athletics coach Geoffrey Dyson, who recognised her hurdling potential. Breaking the British 80 metres hurdle record officially in 1948, Gardner then narrowly missed gold to Fanny Blankers-Koen at the London Olympics that year although she broke both the world and Olympic records with a time of 11.2 seconds. A month after the Olympics she and Dyson were married, and she retired in 1951 to focus on running a ballet school.

# Hester Davenport

1642 – 1717

Actress

**Hester Davenport** (23 March 1642 – 16 November 1717) was an actress, known as Roxalana who called herself the Countess of Oxford. She was a protegée of Sir William and Lady Davenant and appeared in a number of Davenant's company plays, including *Hamlet*, *The Wits* and *Love and Honour*. In 1661 she performed in her most famous role, as Roxalana in a revival of Davenant's *The Siege of Rhodes*. She left the stage the following year, and was reputedly married to Aubrey de Vere, 20th Earl of Oxford. However, she later lost her case to call herself the Countess of Oxford. She appears in a number of the diary entries of Samuel Pepys.

# Dame Bridget D'Oyly Carte
1908 – 1985
Theatre manager

**Dame Bridget D'Oyly Carte** (25 March 1908 – 2 May 1985) was a theatre manager. She was granddaughter to Richard D'Oyly Carte, founder of the D'Oyly Carte Opera Company and controller of the copyrights to the joint works of Gilbert and Sullivan. After her father died in 1948 she inherited the company and became a director of the Savoy Hotel, taking control of furnishing and decoration. She oversaw all new productions, introduced televised and filmed productions, brought in Sir Malcolm Sargent for the 1951 Festival of Britain season and took the company on a series of international tours. After copyrights expired in 1961 she transferred the opera company to a charitable trust, but losses forced the company to close in 1982.

# Celia Franca
1921 – 2007
Ballet dancer, choreographer and ballet director

**Celia Franca** (25 June 1921 – 19 February 2007) was a ballet dancer, choreographer and ballet director. After studying at the Guildhall School of Music and Drama and the Royal Academy of Dance she joined the Ballet Rambert in 1936. When it closed in 1941 she moved to the Sadler's Wells company, appearing in many notable roles, including the Queen in Robert Helpmann's *Hamlet* and the Prostitute in *Miracle of the Gorbals*. In 1947 she joined the Metropolitan Ballet as soloist and ballet mistress, creating the first two ballets commissioned by the BBC, *Dance of Salome* and *Eve of St Agnes*. In 1950 Ninette de Valois recommended Franca to run a new national Canadian ballet, and from 1951 to 1974 she was artistic director, based in Toronto.

Theatre and Live Entertainment

# Florence Farr
## 1860 – 1917
### Actress, author, activist and leader of an occult order

**Florence Farr** (7 July 1860 – 29 April 1917) was an actress, author, activist and leader of an occult order. A childhood friend of May Morris, she posed with her for Burne Jones' painting *The Golden Stairs*. As an actress her presence and voice was noted by George Bernard Shaw and William Butler Yeats who went on to write *Arms and the Man* and *The Land of Heart's Desire* for plays she produced at the Avenue Theatre in London. Considered a 'new woman' she advocated equality for women in *Modern Woman; her intentions*. During the 1890s she was closely involved with The Hermetic Order of the Golden Dawn. After resigning she joined the Theosophical Society and in 1912 left England to become principal of the Ramanathan College in Jaffna, Ceylon.

# Linda Smith

1958 – 2006

Comedian

**Linda Smith** (29 January 1958 – 27 February 2006) was a comedian. After studying English and Drama at Sheffield University she co-formed the community theatre group Sheffield Popular Productions and did many benefit gigs to support the miners during the 1984 to 1985 strike. After moving to London she became a regular on the radio comedy panel shows *The News Quiz, Just a Minute* and *I'm Sorry, I haven't a Clue* and on television programmes such as *Have I got News for You*. She wrote and starred in her own Radio 4 sitcom *Linda Smith's A Brief History of Timewasting*. Smith was president of the British Humanist Association and had a humanist funeral after her death at the age of forty-eight after being diagnosed with ovarian cancer four years earlier.

# Ginny, Lady Fiennes
1947 – 2004
Polar explorer and expedition organiser

**Ginny, Lady Fiennes** (9 July 1947 – 20 February 2004) was a polar explorer and expedition organiser. She met Ranulph Fiennes when she was nine and he twelve; they got married in 1970. She focussed on organising expeditions with her husband. The first was hovercrafting up the White Nile, followed by a 3,000 mile Headless Valley expedition through the Canadian Rockies and four expeditions to find the lost city of Ubar in Dhofar. Their most ambitious project saw Ginny suggesting to travel to both poles along the Greenwich meridian, undertaken between 1979 and 1982 alongside Ginny's scientific work on low frequency radio propagation, for which she became the first woman member of the Antarctic Club. In the 1980s she became a sheep and cattle farmer.

# Index

# Index

# Index

# Index

# Index

Printed in Great Britain
by Amazon